THE BUILDING OF THE ARK

Genesis 6:1—9:7

As time passed, the wickedness of the Cainites spread and entered the families of the tribe of Seth. There were only a few people who remained faithful to the Lord.

For a long time God patiently watched all that was happening, and what He saw made Him sad. He said to Himself, "I will destroy man from the face of the earth."

Truly the people deserved no mercy; nevertheless God delayed His punishment and gave them 120 years to return to Him and ask His forgiveness.

Among all the wicked people in the world there was a man who pleased God. That man was Noah. Instead of following the bad example of the people around him, he continued to love God, to pray to Him, and to trust in His mercy. God told Noah that He would not always strive to bring the people to repentance. He warned that unless they repented there would come a time when He would send a great flood and destroy every living thing. Again and again Noah warned the people about God's punishment, but they paid no attention to him. They were set in their sinful ways, and their thinking and doing continued to be evil.

But God wanted to save Noah and with him his wife, his three sons, and their wives. He told Noah to build a large wooden ark, or ship. It was to be about 450 feet long, 75 feet wide, and 45 feet high. It was to have three decks, each divided into many rooms. They would provide space for the people and the animals that God had planned to save, also space for the storing of food. There was to be a window near the roof and a door in one of its sides. To make the ark watertight, Noah filled the cracks with pitch both inside and outside.

When the ark was finished, God told Noah to go into it with all his family. As for the animals, there was no problem about getting them into the ark, for they came at God's command.

After the people, the animals, and the food were in the ark, God Himself shut the door. Then, after waiting seven days, God sent the flood. Rain began to fall. It came down in torrents. Besides, water gushed up out of the earth. Without letup the water kept coming for 40 days and 40 nights.

How frightened the people must have been when they saw the water getting deeper and deeper! How they must have screamed and rushed to the hills, hoping to find safety there! But there was no way of escape, for eventually the water covered the highest hills. It lifted the ark and made it free to float about on the endless ocean.

At the end of 40 days and nights God stopped the rain. For 150 days the water covered the earth. Then slowly it dried away, and one day the ark stopped floating. It had settled on the ground in the mountains of Ararat.

After 40 days Noah opened the window of the ark and let a raven and a dove fly out. He did this to see whether the ground was dry. The dove returned to the ark. Then Noah knew that the lowland was still covered with water.

A week later Noah again sent out the dove. It returned in the evening, carrying an olive leaf it had picked from a tree. After still another week Noah once more sent out the dove. This time it did not return.

Several weeks later Noah saw that the land was becoming dry, but he stayed in the ark two more months. Then God told Noah and his family to come out of the ark and to bring all the animals with them. Furthermore, God blessed Noah and his family.

Then Noah opened the door of the ark, and he and his family once again stepped on solid ground after living in the ark a year and ten days. The animals also left the ark and began making homes for themselves.

To thank God for sparing him and his family, Noah built an altar and brought a thankoffering to Him. The Lord was pleased with Noah's offering. And He made a wonderful promise. He said, "I will never again send a flood to destroy every living thing. As long as the earth remains, there will always be a seedtime and harvest, cold and heat, summer and winter, day and night."

God put the rainbow into the clouds as a sign and reminder of His promise.

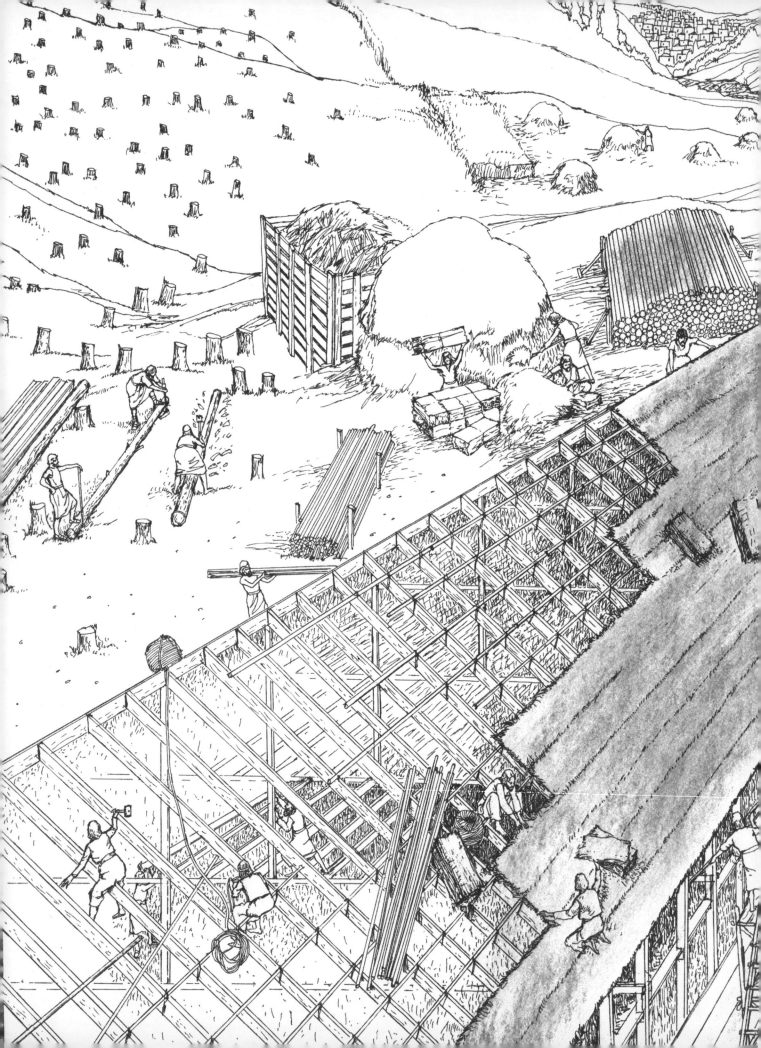

THINGS TO DO

Noah's Incredible Boat

The story of Noah and the flood is a long one—and an exciting one. Fill in the blanks in the following shorter version, using the words listed below it. You won't need one of them.

The Lord saw how _____ everyone on earth had become and was _____ He had made them. "I will _____ them," He decided. But Noah was a _____ man, so God told him to build a _____ out of good _____ and to cover it with _____ . "Take your family and _____ of every _____ and _____ inside with you," said the Lord, "because I am going to send a great _____ ." Noah did as the Lord told him, and soon after it began to _____ . This went on for _____ days and nights till everything drowned. But Noah and everyone with him was safe. After a long time the _____ went away and God put a _____ in the sky.

two	flood	pitch	rain
timber	wicked	good	rainbow
destroy	forty	sorry	bird
water	anchor	animal	boat

A Full-Time Job

Just imagine how much work it must have been to take care of all those animals! How do you think Noah and Mrs. Noah felt when they were able to get off the boat at last? Draw in their faces on the picture below.

Make a Boat

If you're feeling really clever, try making a boat like Noah's—only smaller. Use cardboard you can bend. To be a scale model, the boat should be 45 inches long, 7½ inches wide, and 4½ inches high. It should have a roof, with a tiny space between the roof and the sides, rooms inside, three decks, and a door in the side. And if your boat doesn't turn out looking like Noah's, you can always use it for a flyswatter.

Number Puzzlers

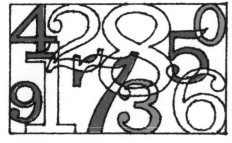

Noah was 600 years old when the flood began. He was 601 years old when it ended. He died at the age of 950. How many years did he live after the flood?.

It rained for 40 days and nights. The water stayed high for 150 days after that. Then it went down for 150 days. Noah waited for 40 more days and then sent out a raven. How long had that raven been in the boat?

Word Search

Try to find all the animal names listed below in the puzzle. You can go up or down, from side to side, or diagonally. Circle each word as you find it. The first one is done for you.

cat	duck	giraffe	tiger
pig	horse	goose	monkey
mouse	rabbit	wasp	

G	I	R	A	F	F	E	
C	G	I	P	M	A	L	
A	E	S	R	O	H	T	
T	A	K	C	U	D	I	
W	G	O	O	S	E	G	
M	O	N	K	E	Y	E	
R	T	I	B	B	A	R	

Make a Rainbow

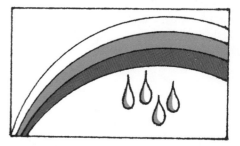

This isn't as hard to do as the boat. Grate crayons (on an old cheese or vegetable grater) and arrange the shavings in arches on a piece of wax paper (waxy side up). Do them in this order: red, orange, yellow, green, blue, purple. Leave about ½ inch between colors. Then put another piece of wax paper over the first one (waxy side down) and iron the two sheets together with a warm iron. The colors will run together a little and you'll have a rainbow to remind you of God's love.

THE BUILDING OF THE TOWER OF BABEL

Genesis 11:1-9

After the great flood, life on earth began anew. At that time everyone spoke the same language. It was possible, therefore, for everyone to understand everyone else. This tended to keep the people together in one place.

Although these people knew about the great flood and why God had sent it, they again turned away from Him. They were proud enough to think they could get along without God. It was His will that they should scatter and fill the earth. But the people said, "Let's build a city and a tower whose top will reach far into the sky. And let us make ourselves famous, so we will not be scattered over the earth."

They found a place to build the city and tower. They used brick for stone and tar, or bitumen, for mortar. Through the labor of many willing hands the city and the tower soon began to take shape.

God took notice of what the people were doing, and what He saw displeased Him greatly. He knew that if the people completed their work, they would become even more sinful—that they would do anything they might want to do.

For this reason the Lord mercifully stopped the people from continuing work on the city and tower. He stopped them by causing them to speak different languages. Since the people could not understand one another, they could not work together. Furthermore, they found it difficult to live together; therefore people who spoke the same language formed a group and moved away to find their own place to live. So the people scattered over the earth, as God had said they should.

The city and the tower the people had been building came to be called Babel, for the Lord had made a "babble," or confusion, of their mixed language.

THINGS TO DO

A Crossword Puzzle

Once everybody spoke the same *1 across*. They wandered around and came to a *2 down*. They decided to bake some *3 across* and put them together with *4 down*. "We will build a *5 down* that will reach the sky," they said. But the Lord did not want them to do that, so He *6 down* up their speech and scattered them all over the *7 across*.

A Hard Job

Making bricks was not easy in Bible times. People had to do everything by hand. The following words all have to do with brickmaking, but they're just a little scrambled.

SKIRBC _____

WARTS _____

NEVO _____

AYCL _____

BEAK _____

RATROM _____

What Did You Say?

Speaking of scrambled, can you imagine what it must have sounded like after God mixed up those people's speech? We don't know what they said exactly, but it must have sounded as confusing as the scrambled sentences below.

Hammer the pass to me.
Foot you my on stepped!
Cold getting tar is the.
We think a problem have I.

Code Message

Another way of scrambling languages is by using code. To break the one used below, circle every fourth letter. The message you'll get is good news in any language!

HALFOTTOBEARHARGAUTOGA R DALSSSNOOHAILALSOGARVBON EGIRDHARTPATHROSESNOW OGL OGEARMARLREADBOATMA THAB BASTATSOTHGENEMARGA NNAM ARVPINEMITHITTIMASSHOBOFAW NCARLANDYMOSSINN OBOON.

Make a Tower

You might like to make a tower that shows how God is more powerful than all the people in the world. Here's one way to do it. Get together a bunch of boxes of different sizes and shapes. Glue or tape them together any way you like—as long as they stand up. Then cut out pictures of people from various countries (newspapers and news magazines are good places to find these) and paste them on the various sides of the boxes. Make a cross out of cardboard and attach it to the top of your tower. You might want to add a sign too, with your decoded message on it.

Language Doesn't Matter

There are times when language does *matter*—like when no one around you speaks yours and you don't speak theirs. But language doesn't matter at all when you talk to God, because He can understand any language. In fact, He can understand what you're praying about even if you don't use language, even if you just sort of open up and share your feelings with Him. Why not spend a few minutes doing that now? It feels great!

ABRAHAM AND THE THREE STRANGERS

Genesis 18:1-16

The day was hot in Mamre. Man and beast eagerly sought relief from the blazing sun. At about noon Abraham sat at the door of his tent, dozing in the shade of some oak trees. When he looked up, he was surprised to see three men standing in front of him. But the three were not really men. Two were angels and the other was the Lord Himself, the Son of God.

Abraham ran at once to meet them. Being a humble, gracious, and hospitable man, he bowed to the earth before them and invited them to be his guests. He said to the Leader of the three, "My Lord, if I have found favor in Your sight, do not pass by me. Let me send for a little water to wash your feet. Then rest yourselves under the tree while I get a bit of food, so you may refresh yourselves."

Abraham hurried into the tent and said to Sarah, "Take some flour and quickly bake some cakes."

Then Abraham ran out into the field and selected a tender calf. He gave it to a servant with orders to prepare meat for the guests. When the meal was ready, Abraham took sour milk and sweet milk, also the veal and the cakes, and set them

before his visitors. He stood near them under a tree while they ate.

When the three had finished their meal, they said to Abraham, "Where is Sarah, your wife?"

Abraham answered, "She is in the tent."

Then the Lord said, "A year from now I will surely return to you and Sarah, your wife, will have a son."

Sarah heard this. She was listening at the door of the tent, behind the Lord. Sarah and Abraham were old. Realizing this, Sarah could not believe that she would have a son; therefore she laughed within herself. Then the Lord, from whom nothing can be hidden, said to Abraham, "Why did Sarah laugh and say, 'Shall I really bear a child, now that I am old?' Is anything too hard for the Lord?"

Sarah became afraid when she saw that the Visitor could read her thoughts. Hoping to defend herself, she lied, saying, "I did not laugh."

Now that the purpose of the visit had been accomplished, Abraham's guests arose and started on their way.

THINGS TO DO

Quite a Surprise

Sarah and Abraham were really surprised by the promise the Lord made to them. Sarah was so surprised that she did something that almost got her in trouble. Fill in the blanks in the story below from the words listed. You won't need three of them.

Abraham was sitting at the _____ of his _____ when he saw three _____ under the _____ . Abraham _____ and asked them to visit. He gave them _____ to wash with and had all sorts of _____ prepared for them. One stranger said, "_____ _____ from now I will come back and your wife Sarah will have a _____ ." When Sarah heard this, she _____ . "I am too _____ ," she thought. "And so is Abraham." Now the Stranger was really the _____ and He heard Sarah. But He kept His _____ anyway.

old	tent	entrance	mouse	laughed	strangers
One	Lord	food	ugly	visit	bowed
trees	year	son	water	promise	

Bible Scene
Abraham and his family lived in tents because their job was raising animals and they had to move around a lot to find enough food for them. It was easier to move a tent than a house, so that's what they did. To make a model of the place where Abraham and Sarah lived, fill a sheet-cake pan with sand or kitty litter. Put in some little branches or plants for trees and a jar lid or soup bowl filled with water for a pond (actually there weren't many of those around). Make your tents out of brightly colored fabric fitted over a pipe-cleaner frame. You might even make pipe-cleaner people and animals for your scene.

Family Trees
Family trees were very important to people of the Bible. Whole chapters tell us who was descended from whom. Bible people were especially proud if they could claim Abraham as their ancestor. And a lot of them could, because God blessed him by giving him many descendants. One of those descendants, in fact, was Jesus! Try to trace your family tree as far back as you can. The following chart might help you.

great-grandfather	great-grandmother	great-grandfather	great-grandmother	great-grandfather	great-grandmother	great-grandfather	great-grandmother

grandfather	grandmother	grandfather	grandmother

father	mother

me

REBEKAH AT THE WELL

Genesis 24

Late one afternoon at the time of Abraham a weary traveler came to a well at the edge of a city. He had 10 camels, a few servants, and some baggage with him. He stopped at the well, alighted from his camel, and knelt down to pray.

This man was Eliezer, Abraham's head servant. He had come to the city of Haran in Mesopotamia to find a God-fearing wife for Isaac, his master's son, who was 40 years old.

He asked God to give him a sign whereby he could tell which of the young women He had chosen to be Isaac's wife. The servant said, "Let the one who will give me water to drink and give water to my camels also be the one whom You have chosen as Isaac's wife."

God answered the man's prayer at once. A lovely young woman named Rebekah came to the well, carrying a water jar on her shoulder. When she had filled her jar, Eliezer went to her and said, "Please give me a little water to drink."

The young woman politely held out her jar and said, "Drink, kind sir."

When the servant had finished drinking, she took the jar and emptied the remaining water into a trough for the camels to drink. Then she drew more water for the camels until there was enough for all of them.

When the camels had finished drinking, the servant opened his baggage and presented Rebekah with two beautiful bracelets and a fine golden nose ring. As he did so, he said, "Tell me whose daughter you are."

Rebekah explained that she was the daughter of a man named Bethuel and the granddaughter of Nahor, Abraham's brother. And she added, "We have straw and food enough for your camels, also room for you."

Eliezer was overjoyed to hear this.

Rebekah ran home and related everything that happened at the well. As soon as Laban, Rebekah's brother, had heard this, he said to Eliezer, "Come in, O blessed of the Lord."

Eliezer went with Laban to the house. There a supper was ready for him.

The members of the family gathered around to listen. Then Eliezer explained why he had come and how God answered his prayer.

Finally the servant asked whether Rebekah would be allowed to go to Canaan with him and marry Isaac. Rebekah's father and brother answered, "It is not for us to say yes or no. There is Rebekah. Take her and go, and let her be the wife of your master's son, for this is the will of the Lord." At once Eliezer thanked God. He gave Rebekah more presents. He also gave rich presents to Rebekah's mother and brother.

The next morning he wanted to start on his way home. The family blessed Rebekah and sent her on her way. Riding on a camel Eliezer had brought, she followed him on the way to Canaan.

Early one evening when the little caravan had come near the place where Abraham and Isaac lived, Isaac was walking in a field. He wanted to be alone, so that he could think quietly about God and worship Him. As he looked up, he saw a train of camels on which Eliezer and his party were riding. Isaac went to meet them.

When Rebekah saw Isaac, she got off her camel and said to Eliezer, "Who is that man coming to meet us?"

The servant said, "It is my master, Isaac."

At once Rebekah covered herself with a veil. It was the proper thing for a lady to do at that time. Then the servant told Isaac all he had done and how God had answered his prayer and sent Rebekah to him. Isaac loved Rebekah. He took her to his tent-home, and they were married.

So it was that God took another step in the fulfillment of His plan to make Abraham the father of a great nation and thus prepare a people among whom the Savior would be born.

THINGS TO DO

A Crossword Puzzle

Abraham sent his *1 down* away from *2 down* to find a *3 down* for his *4 across.* The man went to Mesopotamia and stopped at a *3 across* where he *5 across.* Along came Rebekah. She gave him some *6 down* and drew some for his *7 across* too. She was the *6 across* for *8 across!*

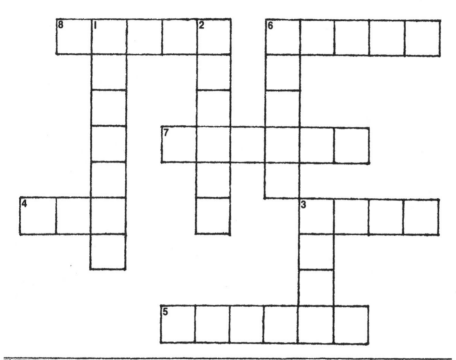

Thirsty Camels

The servant had 10 camels with him and Rebekah gave water to all of them. If her jar held 3 quarts and if each camel drank a gallon, how many times did she have to refill her jar? (Hint: There are 4 quarts in 1 gallon.)

Scrambled Relatives

This Bible story mentions a lot of people who were related to one another. Some of them had names that sound pretty strange to us. See if you can unscramble the following names of the relatives. If you need help, look at Genesis 24.

MARHABA _____

BEETLUH _____

HORAN _____

BLANA _____

CASAI _____

KRABEEH _____

Make Up ★ a Blessing ★

As Rebekah left her home to go to Isaac, her family gave her a blessing. They wished her two things that were very important to people at that time: that she have many descendants and that her descendants would conquer the cities of their enemies. If your family were going to give you a blessing, what would you like them to say? What sort of blessing would you give each of them? You might write these blessings on pieces of paper and share them at dinner sometime. ★

A Powerful Helper

The servant asked God to help him with his important job. Unscramble the words in the first part of the servant's prayer. And remember—you can ask God to help you with the things you have to do too! Let the ENO who will give me TERWA to KRIND and give ERTAW to my MELCAS also be the NOE whom You have chosen as ICASA'S wife.

Make Some Stick Puppets

To make stick puppets, all you have to do is draw and cut out figures from heavy paper and tape them to dowels or sticks or unsharpened pencils. You can kneel behind a table or couch and hold them so they show over the top to put on your puppet show. The pictures below should give you the general idea.

JACOB AND ESAU REUNITED

Genesis 32:3—33:20

Twenty years had passed since Jacob fled from his brother Esau, who had threatened to kill him. As Jacob proceeded on his way home after a long stay with his uncle Laban, he wondered whether Esau had forgiven him, or whether the old hatred still lingered in his heart. To find out, Jacob sent messengers to the land of Edom, where Esau lived.

The messengers found Esau and delivered Jacob's message to him. When the messengers returned, they had bad news to tell. "Esau is coming," they said. "He has 400 men with him."

Immediately Jacob divided his people and his animals into two groups. Then he separated the groups so there would be some distance between them. Jacob did this thinking: If Esau meets one group and destroys it, the other group will have a chance to escape.

In his distress Jacob prayed, saying, "O God of my fathers, You told me to return to my home. You also promised to be good to me. I am not worthy of all the kindness and faithfulness with which You have favored me. When I crossed the Jordan River on my way to Haran, I had nothing but my staff. Now my possessions make two large companies. Save me, I pray You, from my brother, for I fear he is coming to kill us all."

The next day Jacob gathered 580 animals of various kinds as a present for Esau. Jacob told his servants to keep the animals of each kind as a separate group when they drove them to Esau, and to drive the groups one behind the other, leaving some space between them.

Before the shepherds started on their way, Jacob said to them, "When Esau meets you and asks whose animals you have, say to him, 'They belong to Jacob. He is sending them as a present to my lord Esau. Jacob is close behind us.'"

When it was morning, Jacob joined his family on the far side of the river. Soon he noticed Esau and his 400 men coming toward him. Jacob went out alone to meet him. As he approached his brother, he bowed to the ground seven times. He thought that this might help appease Esau's anger. But Esau wasn't angry anymore, for God had changed his heart. He ran to meet Jacob, took him lovingly into his arms, and kissed him. Then the brothers wept for joy.

Esau looked up and saw the women and children with Jacob. "Who are these?" he asked.

"They are the ones whom God has graciously given to me," Jacob said.

Then Esau asked, "What did you mean by sending the droves of animals I met?"

Jacob told Esau that he had sent them as a gift in the hope that it would make his heart favorable toward him. At first Esau refused the gift, but when Jacob urged him, he accepted it.

Then Esau suggested that his people and Jacob's people travel the rest of the way together. This would make it possible for Esau and his men to protect Jacob and his family. But Jacob saw no need for such protection. Besides, he feared that his flocks and herds, especially the young among them, would not be able to keep up with Esau and his men. If they were driven too hard, many would die.

After the brothers said good-bye, Esau returned to his home in Edom, and Jacob went on to Canaan.

THINGS TO DO

Praise God!

During Bible times, people often made a simple altar to mark a place where God had been good to them. Noah did that after the flood was over, and Jacob did it at Peniel where he had wrestled with God. Mostly we have altars in our churches now, but there are other ways of reminding ourselves to praise God for His goodness.

For example, you could make a banner. Cut the background out of felt or heavy colored paper. (The picture below will give you one idea of how to do this.) Then cut out shapes or words or pictures that remind you of God's goodness to you and paste them onto your background. Fod the tabs at the top of the banner over a dowel or stick and tape or staple them down. Attach string or yarn and then hang your banner in a place that is special to you.

More Relatives

Lots of stories in the Bible are about pairs of brothers and sisters. See how many you can match together in the following lists.

Cain	Benjamin	Peter
Mary	Shem	Joseph
Ham	Leah	Abel
Rachel	Andrew	Martha

What's Your Name?

In Bible times people chose names for their children that meant something very specific. We think that Jacob's name meant "heel," because he was born holding onto his brother's heel. Esau was a very hairy baby and his name probably means "hairy." When God changed Jacob's name, He called him "Israel," which probably means "he struggles with God." Do you know what your name means? Try looking it up in a book of names for baby or in the back of a dictionary to find out. If you could choose your own name, one that would tell something about you, what name would you choose?

Number Puzzlers

Jacob sent his brother 200 female goats, 20 male goats, 200 female sheep, 20 male sheep, 30 milk camels with their young, 40 cows, 10 bulls, 20 female donkeys, and 10 male donkeys. If half of the camels each had a baby camel, how many animals did Jacob send in all?

If Jacob divided the animals into herds according to their breed and put one servant in charge of each herd and if he had 20 servants to begin with, how many servants were left to take care of his family and the rest of his animals?

The Dirty Trick

Do you know how Jacob and Esau got separated in the first place? Well, Jacob played a very dirty trick on Esau in order to get his father's blessing. You can read all about that in Genesis 27. Actually, most of the people we think of as heroes or heroines in the Bible did something pretty bad or foolish at one time or another in their lives. Unscramble the names of the following Bible people and try to remember what they did. Only one of them was a perfect hero. Put a circle around that name.

VIDDA _____

POSHEJ _____

RATHAM _____

HEJAIL _____

OMESS _____

RYMA _____

MOONSLO _____

LAPU _____

JUSSE _____

RASHA _____

Strong Feelings

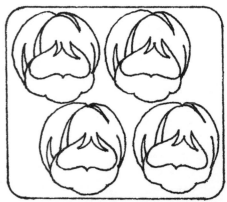

Draw in faces that show how Jacob was feeling in the following situations: (1) when he played the trick on his brothers; (2) when he had to run away and live all alone; (3) when he found out Esau was coming to meet him with 400 men; (4) when Esau hugged him.

JOSEPH SOLD INTO SLAVERY

Genesis 37:1

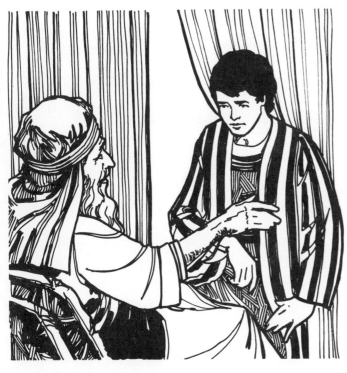

Serious trouble arose in the family of Jacob. Among the older brothers there developed a hatred for Joseph.

When Joseph was 17 years old, he worked in the fields with his older brothers. They tended their father's flocks at Hebron. At times Joseph saw his brothers doing wicked things, and he told his father about them. This made the brothers hate Joseph. And soon something happened that increased their hatred.

Father Jacob loved Joseph more than any of his other children, because Joseph was born when Jacob was old and because he was the son of his beloved wife Rachel. Jacob gave Joseph a fine robe. When Joseph's brothers saw that their father loved Joseph more than any of them, they became very jealous and very angry.

Later something happened that made them hate Joseph even more. Joseph had a dream, and he told it to his brothers. He said, "In my dream we were in a field trying grain into bundles. My bundle stood up straight. But your bundles gathered around my bundle and bowed down to it."

In this dream God foretold that someday Joseph would rule over his brothers. But the brothers thought it showed that Joseph was proud and wanted to lord it over them. They said to him, "Do you really think you are going to be a king?"

Joseph had another dream. This time when he told it, his father was present. "I dreamed," Joseph said, "that the sun, the moon, and eleven stars were bowing down to me."

Even father Jacob was upset by this dream. He scolded Joseph, saying, "Must I, your mother, and your brothers bow ourselves to the ground before you?"

But Jacob could not forget the dream.

There came a time when the 10 oldest brothers took their father's flock about 50 miles north to feed on the grass near a place called Shechem. Days and weeks passed, but Jacob received no word from his sons. Rather worried, Jacob called Joseph and said, "Go and see if all is well with your brothers and the flock. Then return and tell me how they are getting along."

The brothers saw Joseph coming in the distance. At once they planned to get rid of him. "Look," they said "here comes the dreamer. Let us kill him and throw him into a pit here in the wilderness. We will tell our father that some wild animal killed him. Then we shall see what will become of his dreams."

All agreed to the plan except Reuben, the oldest brother. He tried to find a way to save Joseph. He said, "Let's not hurt Joseph. We'll just throw him into a pit and leave him there."

Reuben meant to rescue Joseph when they were alone and return him safe to his father.

The brothers liked Reuben's idea. And so, when Joseph came near, they grabbed him, tore off his beautiful robe, and let him down into an empty cistern. Without paying any attention to Joseph's cries for mercy, the brothers calmly sat down and ate their lunch.

After a while they saw a group of men on camels coming their way. It was a caravan of Ishmaelite traders going to Egypt. The camels were loaded with large bundles of spices and perfumes, which the Ishmaelites were taking to market. These traders gave Judah, the fourth oldest brother, a new idea about getting rid of Joseph. "What will we gain by killing Joseph?" he said. "Let us sell him as a slave."

The other brothers quickly agreed. When the Ishmaelites were near, they bargained with them awhile and then sold Joseph to them for 20 silver coins. The Ishmaelites took Joseph with them to Egypt.

Reuben was not around when Joseph was sold. Imagine how he felt when he went to the pit to take Joseph out and saw that he was not there. Beside himself with grief, Reuben ran to the brothers and said, "The boy is gone! Where shall I go?"

The brothers told Reuben what they had done. But how could they explain Joseph's disappearance to their father? Quickly they found a way. They killed a goat, dipped Joseph's robe in its blood, and had a messenger take it to their father with orders to say, "We found this. See whether it is your son's robe."

Jacob recognized it at once. "It is my son's robe," he said. "A wild beast has torn Joseph to pieces."

Crushed with grief, Jacob tore his clothes, wore sackcloth, and mourned for Joseph many days. All his family tried to comfort Jacob, but he refused to be comforted. He said, "I shall go down into the grave mourning for my son."

THINGS TO DO

A Limerick

Here's a limerick for you to finish. The last line should have the same rhythm as the first two and should rhyme with them.

**There once was a young lad called Joe,
Whose brothers all hated him so.
One day in a twit,
They found a deep pit.**

_____

Family Problems

When you stop to think about it, Joseph's brothers had a lot of reasons not to like him very much. Try to keep track of them as you fill in the blanks in the following version of the story. The words you'll need are listed below, but you won't need three of them.

Joseph took care of the _____ and _____ with his brothers and brought bad _____ to his _____ about what the brothers were doing. Jacob _____ Joseph more than his other _____, so he made a special _____ for him. Once Joseph had a dream in which they were all tying up _____ of _____ in the field. Joseph's bundle _____ up straight and the others formed a _____ and _____ down to it. Another time Joseph dreamed that the _____, the _____, and _____ bowed down to him. He told his brothers about these dreams and they didn't like them—not one bit!

father	circle	goats	loved	cows	eleven
pumpkins	sheep	wheat	sheaves	bowed	sun
robe	stars	moon	sons	stood	reports

Super Duds

From what we're told, that robe of Joseph's must have been something else! The picture of it below is for you to color.

Make a Joseph Doll

Word Search

Try to find all the people and place names listed below in the puzzle. You can go up or down, from side to side, or diagonally. Circle each word as you find it.

Jacob   Dothan   Egypt   Shechem
Joseph   Reuben   Judah

J	A	C	O	B	H	S
R	O	N	N	A	B	H
L	E	S	D	O	N	E
R	B	U	E	R	A	C
A	J	O	B	P	A	H
T	P	Y	G	E	H	E
D	O	T	H	A	N	M

A Tongue Twister

Try to get your tongue around this one three times—fast.

Baby brother bragged and boasted to brawny, blustering big brothers.

Start with a plain wooden clothespin and paint on a face. Wrap a pipe-cleaner around the neck to form arms. Cut a hole in the center of a rectangle of fabric and place it over the head. Tie it around the waist with a piece of yarn to form a robe. Glue on yarn or a piece of ball fringe for hair. You've got a Joseph!